Instructor
Missionary
Miriam Knox

May God richly
bless you & warm your
heart as you read the
poetry within. Thank you

Gail M. Frahone

FROM WITHIN

*A Collection of Simple Inspirational Poetry
for a "Not-So-Simple" World*

by

Gail Mahome

AuthorHouse™
1663 Liberty Drive, Suite 200
Bloomington, IN 47403
www.authorhouse.com
Phone: 1-800-839-8640

© *2008 Gail Mahome. All rights reserved.*

No part of this book may be reproduced, stored in a retrieval system, or transmitted by any means without the written permission of the author.

First published by AuthorHouse 3/5/2008

ISBN: 978-1-4343-4564-6 (sc)

Cover design by Evangelist A. Henderson
"Altar Prayer" - McGee Temple COGIC
Chicago, Illinois

Printed in the United States of America
Bloomington, Indiana

This book is printed on acid-free paper.

DEDICATION

To Mildred I. Anson, a light that continuously shines in my life. A true child of God. I love you Momma.

SPECIAL THANKS AND ACKNOWLEDGEMENTS

Above everything, I am blessed to be able to give thanks to my Heavenly Father, in the name of my Lord, Jesus Christ. For it is through Him and Him alone that this vision was unfolded and has come to completion. Without God, this book would have never been possible. To God be the glory in Christ Jesus.

To my dearly beloved brother, Reginald Gunter, who out of his love for God, and all of God's creation, labored diligently to edit, critique and conform all that was written for the edification of the saints of God and to reach a lost world. You are phenomenal in your obedience, perseverance and commitment to the Word of God. God has truly blessed me to have you as my brother earthly and spiritually. I love you and may God continue to bless you.

To three dynamic women: Doretha Jordan, Lynn Rowland and Vanessa Yvette Williams. Doretha for seeing the vision before I did and in obedience encouraged me to use the gift that God had so graciously bestowed upon me. Lynn for the listening ear, for it was you who first heard almost every poem after the Spirit of the Lord had given them to me. Vanessa for your encouragement and support, in addition to lifting up the name of the Lord during some rough times. You all are valuable friends and I am once again blessed to have each of you in my life.

To my most beloved Pastor and First Lady; Elder Willie & Fannie Henderson for their guidance, support and prayers through this project.

Additionally, to my church family, the McGee Temple Church of God in Christ for their prayers, love and support.

To Pastor Robert and First Lady Leangela Aitken of True Light Baptist Church for all their efforts in keeping me focus on this project. Thank you and I appreciate all that you have done for me.

To my family and the many friends who have supported me every step of the way. I love you all.

TABLE OF CONTENTS

Dedication v
Special Thanks And Acknowledgements................................ vii
Table of Contents ix
Introduction xi

RECOGNITION

Recognition 3
A Place To Be 4
Bless Him 5
Blessed Three 6
Burn Spirit, Burn 8
Deliverance 9
He's Faithful 10
He's Still God 11
I Praise You 12
My Wonderful Savior 13
Small Things 14
The God You Serve 15
Trusting Jesus 16
We Thank You 17
Why Do I Love Him? 18
With Outstretched Arms 19

REALITY

Reality 23
A Believer's World 24
Be Ready 25

Conquering Temptation 26
Don't Stop 27
Faith 28
Going To God 29
He Found Me 31
My Cry 32
My Rescue 33
Needing God 34
Pray 35
Rededication 36
Soul Surrender 38
Stepping Aside 39
That Day 40
The Battle 42
The Journey 43
The Voice 45
Where Are You? 46

REMEMBRANCE

Remembrance 51
A Leader For God 52
Discipleship 53
He Heals 54
Her Destiny 56
King David 58
The Apostle 60
The Dreamer 61
Three Determined Men 63
What Adam Had 65

INTRODUCTION

FROM WITHIN is a book of inspirational poetry. It expresses the love and reverence that a believer has for God; it reaches deep into situations, trials and circumstances that we as humans experience everyday; and it recalls to our memories those who truly knew God as Lord and Savior. **FROM WITHIN** has been written to lovingly inspire, encourage and offer hope to those who want to understand, know and have a relationship with the all-mighty, all-powerful, ever present God of this universe, through His Son, our Lord and Savior, Jesus Christ.

FROM WITHIN is comprised of a combination of poems, ranging from praise and worship to spiritual testimonies and experiences; as well as, biblical attributes. The rhyming style of writing was chosen in order to offer simplicity and easy reading for individuals of all ages. It is hoped, to the glory of God, that **FROM WITHIN** touches the life of each and every reader, giving them a hunger and a thirst deep within their spirit for the Word of God.

RECOGNITION

RECOGNITION

Webster's Dictionary says that "**recognition**" is the action of recognizing; the state of being recognized; special notice or attention.

Some of the most important questions we could ask ourselves are: How do we view God? What do we feel deep down inside about our Creator? Do we realize that God is awesome, always near, all-powerful, knows everything, owns everything, made everything and is holy? Do we believe that only He can give peace that surpasses all understanding? Do we know that He is Love?(1) For He loved us so much that He sent His only Son to die for us that we may live with Him for eternity.

The following poems express the love, fear and praise that one should bestow in acknowledgement of the great "I AM." The Holy Trinity: God the Father, God the Son, and God the Holy Spirit. It is my desire that you humbly open your heart, soul and spirit as you read the poetry in this section as they offer praise and worship to triune the Holy Trinity. The Word of God says: "Let everything that has breath, praise the Lord."(2)

(1)   St. John 3:16
(2)   Psalm 150:6

A PLACE TO BE

There are so many changes
    Uncertain directions in my life
My spirit gets uneasy
    I know this pressure must be strife
I have found a special place
    That my troubled soul can go
It's a place of rest and peace
    Full of comfort that I know

As long as I am there
    I never have a need to grumble
My life has sweet serenity
    My spirit is meek and humble
Here I get to see things
    With blessed spiritual eyes
I share God's love and His kindness
    Never hatred or sinful lies

At this place, nothing seems to stir
    Feeling like the quiet before the storm
But I have no fear within me
    I am protected, my heart is warm
God leads me through this place
    Sometimes He says be still
It is only at this place
    That I'm in the center of His will

BLESS HIM

The store, the waves, the thunder, changing the course of natural things.
Only my Blessed Savior can truly speak, calming the friction
    that life brings.
As I give Him everything, that comes my way throughout the day.
He tells the evil to leave my presence, for it's only Him all must obey.

I know that He's my Savior, I can't survive life on my own..
His words are secure within my heart; I know I'm not alone.
He's my ever-present help, when things are out of control.
He strengthens me and guides me; bringing comfort to my soul.

He is faithful and forgiving; when I repent because I've done wrong.
He shows me love and amazing grace; it's with Him that I belong.
How great He is in mercy; giving peace I can't explain.
He shall reign in my heart forever and I say bless His Holy Name.

BLESSED THREE

The Almighty God is our Father
   With Jesus, His Son, by His side (1)
The Holy Spirit dwelling within us
   As our Comforter and our Guide
Witnessing such an amazing union (2)
   What a marvelous thing it is to see
Shekinah glory, power and love
   Within the Holy Trinity
When Jesus spoke on prayer
   He said, "Thy kingdom come" (3)
He also said these awesome words
   "I and My Father are One" (4)
This astounding splendor before us
   Reigning from the heavens above
It's comprised of something incredible
   It's agape, it is love
As it is written, the Word became flesh (5)
   It also became our precious sacrifice
None on earth, only Jesus from heaven
   Could pay the ultimate price
The Father's unyielding love
   Giving His Son who lived and died (6)
He defeated death by arising
   Showing love the Father wouldn't hide
With the Trinity there is holiness
   Righteousness and truth
With creating power and healing power
   And resurrection as it's proof

They are omniscient and infinite
    By His Spirit we can perceive
God inspired men to write His words
    We need only to believe
The Father, who spoke all things into creation
    Jesus, the Lord and Savior of us all

With the Holy Spirit fully active
    To answer each and every call
Yes, the Holy Trinity is overwhelming
    Captivating and glorious as can be
We receive love, grace and mercy
    When we embrace the Blessed Three

(1) Luke 3:21, 22

(2) 1st John 5:7, 8

(3) Matthew 6:10

(4) St. John 10:30

(5) St. John 1:14

(6) Romans 5:8

BURN SPIRIT, BURN

Holy Spirit, I ask You
For You have been of old
Please consume me like fire
To the core of my soul

Singe away the evil
So my life can be sweet
My life, Your example
Of one of God's greatest feats

Holy Spirit, without You
I know I will perish
Stay with me, I need You
Your love I will cherish

Convict me, love me
Show me Your ways
I'll bless You, won't grieve You
All of my days

Holy Spirit, I thank You
For You've heard my call
I welcome Your coming
I give You my all

Your presence within me
Will cause a great turn
For entwined within my spirit
Your love for me will burn

DELIVERANCE

Your Savior, Your Redeemer
The just and faithful One
He brings deliverance just for you
Jesus, the Father's only begotten Son
He gives you life, because He is life
Even when temptations block your view
No matter what the enemy brings your way
Jesus is there to deliver you
Let those with ears, clearly listen
Open your eyes and you shall see
Quietly sit and patiently wait
For He will deliver thee
Doing what seems impossible
For the children that He loves
Upon surrender, there's deliverance
Sweet victory from above
Lift your hands high in the air
Thank God and give Him praise
For there is no end to His graciousness
And His awesome delivering ways
Exalt Him for He's your Deliverer
Look forward to better days
Grasp hold of this new freedom
Look towards Jesus as you do
This is your chance to live again
For He's provided deliverance just for you

HE'S FAITHFUL

Many circumstances come that weigh us down
Obstacle block our way and we feel that we're bound
But there's Someone who'll remove things our of our way
He will give us the strength to face everyday
No matter what this old world will try to do
He is faithful and just to see us through
We may stumble a bit, we might even fall
But if we cry out to Him, He'll answer each call
Jesus, our King, our Bright Morning Star
Will come to our aid not matter how far
He'll come when we call and stay by our side
If we bring all to Him with nothing to hide
So as trials and tribulations come into view
We'll trust that only Jesus will know what to do
When the enemy has plans to do us great harm
We'll rest faithfully and safely in Jesus' arms

HE'S STILL GOD

It doesn't matter who you know or where you have been

God is still the same God

Praise Him for deliverance or confess your deepest sin

God is still the same God

When you pray for things and don't understand

God is still the same God

He'll only give you an answer according to His plan

For God is still the same God

He never slumbers, nor changes, nor tells any lies

His ears are always open to all of your cries

No matter how difficult this world may seem to be

You must stay rooted in Jesus and you will see

That if you stay armored up and your feet are well shod
You'll know for sure and understand, that
God is still the same God

I PRAISE YOU

I praise You, I praise You
    I praise Your holy name
There's no other joy
    That I can say is the same

Right before my eyes
    Your greatness unfolds
My wonderful Creator
    Your love I behold

You are merciful and awesome
    And so full of grace
My all-knowing God
    None can ever take Your place

Your boundaries are endless
    They stretch all around
Anywhere in the universe
    Your presence is found

I worship You, adore You
    I love You so much
You're my life, my all
    I embrace Your touch

As I come into Your presence
    On a bended knee
I praise You, my God
    With all that's in me

MY WONDERFUL SAVIOR

His death and resurrection; something that had to be
I'm talking about my Savior, Jesus
It brought eternal salvation to both you and me
I'm talking about my Savior, Jesus
He lived and preached compassion and love
I'm talking about my Savior, Jesus
He provided the way to our Father above
I'm talking about my Savior, Jesus
From birth to death, He lived sin free
I'm talking about my Savior, Jesus
He's the greatest example that there ever will be
I'm talking about my Savior, Jesus
When the world cried for a Savior, they thought God forgot
But when He arrived on the scene they knew Him not
Oh, but He arrived and many have thus been saved
They just didn't know He'd come as a Babe
I'm talking about my Savior, Jesus

SMALL THINGS

Oh God!

What can I thank You for today?
Maybe just for the little things You brought my way

Small pretty birds, a little child's smile
Or just to kick up my heels, and rest for a while

The smell of sweet flowers or blossoming trees
Lifting my face to the sky and feeling the breeze

Someone else's laughter, the sight of joyful tears
Even the gentle way You wash away all of my fears

There are so many glorious things
For which I often pray

God, I just want to thank You
For the little things today!!

Thanks God

THE GOD YOU SERVE

As adversity comes before you
    You get confused and don't know why
Unexpected turmoil begins to surface
    Causing your soul within to cry
There are answers to these problems
    You must search deep inside yourself
Let the Holy Spirit be your strength
    For there's some fight in you that's left
Start with self-encouragement
    Give thanks and pray for your life today
Don't be afraid to take you stand
    Then boldly this is what you say:
The God I serve hears all my cries
The God I serve is much alive
The God I serve loves me dearly
He gave His Son and I know He hears me
The God I serve has all the power
He stays with me through every hour
The God I serve is always around
I depend on Him, He won't let me down
The God I serve has set me free
For He's the God who created Me
When I feel weak and my heart can't sing
When the cares of the world has trouble to bring
I'll run to shelter of His almighty wings
For only the God I serve can do all things

TRUSTING JESUS

A lie He won't tell
    Because of who He is
That's one of the reasons I trust Him
He will not change,
    For the world is His
That's one of the reasons I trust Him
When I tell Him my secrets
    No one will He tell
That's one of the reasons I trust Him
He died on the cross
    To keep me from Hell
That's one of the reasons I trust Him
When I'm alone at night and can't fall asleep
    Surrounded by darkness, my soul starts to weep
Like the shepherd, He comes protecting His sheep
    Staying faithful to me, His promises He keeps

These are the reasons I trust Him

WE THANK YOU

We thank You dear Father
    For all the wonders You've done
For Your sweet saving grace
    And the blood of Your Son
We know in our hearts
    That You're before the beginning
The Almighty great "I AM"
    Who has not an ending
It is only in Your image
    That we were created from the dust
We thank You for we know
    You breathed life into us
Everything is from You
    Jehovah, this we understand
We thank You for Your love
    Over and over again
We exalt You, O' God
    Yes, above everything
We worship and praise You
    For Your glory we sing
As we look to the heavens
    We say, Holy God, thank You
With the highest of honors
    We thank only You

WHY DO I LOVE HIM?

Do you know why I love Him?
    I love Him because of the road He paved
    He made a great sacrifice especially for me
    To insure my soul would be saved
Do you know why I love Him?
    Because for hours He hung at Calvary
    He experienced a gruesome and lonely death
    To remove sin's bondage from me
Do you know why I love Him?
    Because He stepped in and He took my place
    Showing me something that I didn't know
    All God's love, mercy and saving grace
Do you know why I really love Him?
    It's because He was sent from God above
    He did something for me that no one else could do
    And He did it all out of love

That's why I love Him!!!

WITH OUTSTRETCHED ARMS

I lift my hands very high in the air
      I've stretched them upward and straight
To my God, who I know is there
      At the opening of heaven's gate
Allowing my eyes to look only forward
      To the great openness of heavenly space
While meditating my mind envisions
      Looking into my Lord's awesome face
The door to my heart is completely open
      Concerned with only matters from above
By opening the door, I know I'll receive
      Every drop of my Savior's love
So I'll keep my feet firmly planted
      Not allowing the enemy to shake me free
For I stand in the presence of God Almighty
      And there's no other place I'd rather be

REALITY

REALITY

Webster's Dictionary says that **"reality"** is the quality or state of being real. The totality of real things or events.

As I have read through different books of the Bible; I learned that Jacob saw a ladder, Ezekiel saw a wheel, and the disciples saw Jesus walk on the Sea of Galilee. As we become new creatures in Christ, many of us will experience different powerful revelations that show we have crossed over from non-believer to believer. We come to the knowledge that what we experienced was very real and it becomes a part of our testimony.

The poetry in this section convey such experiences. They express how a cry of despair becomes a cry of triumph in Christ; how doubt and fear can be turned into hope and faith; showing how only God can produce victory for all of our battles. As you read, may you proclaim what the Apostle Paul proclaimed when he said: "I press toward the mark for the prize of the high calling of God in Christ Jesus." (1)

(1) Philippians 3:14

A BELIEVER'S WORLD

The life of a believer is not easy
    It begins with hills and mountains to climb
We can only survive by clinging to Jesus
    Because we're the branch and He's the Vine
Uncertain paths we often travel
    Perilous storms may cause us to weep
Should we become weary and lose our way
    We know He's the Shepherd who finds His sheep

Old habits and negative thoughts
    Are replaced with persistent love
Bringing our lives great joy and peace
    Which are fruit from God above
The carnal way we use to live
    Dies and we bravely take the lost
We give God praise, glory and thanks
    For Jesus' victory at the cross

The adversary wants to hinder us
    In every way to turn us around
We take heed from the words of Jesus
    By being sown on very good ground
We have to walk away from temptation
    Avoiding confusion, envy and strife
This is because we've been born again
    Having put to death our previous life

Although the road for us is tedious
    Our Lord Jesus suffered the greatest pain
He lived sinlessly, then was crucified
    So eternal life we could attain
As believers we continue to press onward
    For there'll be crowns and much reward
We'll receive a life that will last forever
    In the presence of our Lord

BE READY

I know this for sure
  It's an already given fact
That my Lord lived, died, arose
  And is surely coming back
He's the Bridegroom who has done
  A pure and soulful search
He's returning to this earth
  For His bride, the Church
I don't know which season,
  Nor the month, day or hour
Only that it will be very quick
  And He'll have all the power
Get ready, O Church
  For it's time to apprehend
All the lost hearts and souls
  Of this world's women and men
We cannot take this for granted
  For this will not be a test
We must get ourselves ready
  For this glorious harvest
He's most definitely coming
  In the twinkling of an eye
If we're not watching and praying
  It will surely pass us by
From heaven He will come
  Yes, the Lamb that was slain
He'll eradicate sickness and death
  Torture, heartache and pain
I'm going to do what it takes
  To be a part of this, you see
For when my Lord returns to earth
  I want Him to come back for me

CONQUERING TEMPTATION

I am tempted and attacked, but I put up a very strong fight
By studying and praying; by doing what is right
I see deception, feel rejection. Many, many lies I have heard
I don't care what comes my way; I stand only on God's Word
Although it may sound good and be pleasing to my eyes
I learn each day to die to my flesh, so it will never rise
Yes, sometimes it's very difficult to keep myself under control
The Holy Spirit has the help I need; empowering my spirit and my soul
I believe that good will triumph over every bad ordeal
Because I know that for my life; God has a purpose and a will
As Jesus was God wrapped in flesh and lived the righteous way
I only pray for understanding and the spirit to obey

DON'T STOP

Many decisions will be made
    On all the things that you must do
Just trust all of His promises
    Because all of them are true
He knows where you are going
    Before you even begin to step out
You have to leave everything to Him
    And must never-ever doubt

As you approach each situation
    Another will be waiting there for you
Keep all your focus on your Savior
    For it is He that will see you through
Hold on tight to all your courage
    Try very hard not to slip
By standing only on God's Word
    You will never lose your grip

You must rebuke the negative things
    That try to block your way
Then concentrate, meditate
    Or simply kneel and pray
You must refuse to be shaken
    By anything that is around
Never stop looking towards the Master
    And you will never lose your ground

Press confidently through your circumstances
    No matter what to you is said
He'll prepare you with His grace
    For whatever storm that lies ahead
Every single day that you face
    Will be much easier to live
Just never ever stop giving Him
    All that you can give

FAITH

If in your heart you honestly know
And you really, really truly believe
That everything comes from God
Available for you to receive
In your mind there are no questions
No room for any doubt
Your actions will surely show
What your faith is all about

With the will to patiently wait
That removes the sense of worry
Your hope must remain alive
Never a need to be in a hurry
The situation will manifest itself
There'll be praises to sing at last
Because you have kept your faith
The thing will surely come to pass

Faith comes from deep within
Not a personal want or simple wish
It's believing all that God has said
And standing on every promise
Faith is what is hoped for
Anticipation of things to come
Understanding that God is the Rewarder
Of where all things must come from

As your are looking at your life
At many things you cannot see
Sometimes pondering and wondering
How some things will really be
If you remove all self-indulgence
Never giving place to any doubt
Obeying and trusting the Lord
You'll find what faith is all about

GOING TO GOD

A time comes to make a special trip
    To the most precious throne of grace
The condition of our spirit cries
    It's now the perfect place
Being the only place we know
    That can handle our desperate pleas
Straight to the presence of our Savior
    Down on our bended knees
We give the soulish cry for help
    Relinquishing all that's in our hands
Letting Him pick up every burden
    Then reworking all our plans
It wasn't meant for us to bear
    These things all by ourselves
Our Heavenly Father, our Creator
    Has provided us with help
We are human and we're limited
    But the Blessed Holy Spirit is not
He's mighty and He's powerful
    Or is that something we've forgot

He's an ever present help
>	When we think we're all alone
He takes us to the Father
>	When we must approach the throne
God knows before we come
>	What we need as we draw near
He has all the answers for us
>	We just need a listening ear
For some trials are merely tests
>	Some tribulations, a simple quiz
Often needed just to determine
>	If we are really, truly His
As we reach deep down inside
>	Giving Him our troubles from within

He'll replace it with His love
>	And a charge to begin again
Divine guidance will be given
>	It will be sweet music to our souls
We need only to let Christ be our Lord
>	By giving Him complete control

HE FOUND ME

Living a life so full of pain
Doing things, receiving no gain
Always walking on shaky ground
Stability for me could not be found

But He always found me

Looking for answers and finding none
Feeling inside that all hope was gone
My quest was to find only the right way
A place of peace where my soul could stay

He still took time to find me

Searching for love in all the wrong places
Surviving on glimpses, pieces and traces
Not really knowing what I was looking for
All the time Jesus was right at my door

He knew exactly where to find me

At my lowest point, when I needed a friend
I opened the door and Jesus came in
He brightened the light in my heart
That was so very, very dim
It was right at that moment

That I found Him

MY CRY

Dear Lord,
I come to You because I know that You care
You know everything about me
Please hear my prayer
Don't turn me away Lord
Please hear me, please
Cleanse my heart and my soul
Of their sinful deeds
Remove all the things, Lord
I know that You hate
Restore my life, O God
Make all my paths straights
Control my thoughts
Each and every move that I make
Help me, please God
For Jesus' sake
I'm crying unto You, God
With all of my might
Bring me out of the darkness
Into Your marvelous light
Take my spirit, please God
Guide it and show it the way
From the innermost parts of me, Lord
This, my cry, I pray

MY RESCUE

My darkened soul falls into the evil of the night
Once again I am rescued from this sickening plight
How often must I go there? Only to be saved
Am I drawing closer and closer to the pit of my grave?
I get entangled, ensnared by this captivating thing
But then, deliverance comes and I joyfully sing
With the voice of thankfulness I sing to God a new song
Encamped near me is wickedness, but His strength makes me strong
My enemies, they stalk me, I hear the lion's loud roar
He raises me above them, like a proud eagle I soar
I am rescued again, from this most menacing prey
I find peace in my heart, under God's wings I will stay
Should I ever feel I'm falling, drowning or loosing it all
Searching for answers and to this world I do call
The right responses won't come, for surely this I must do
Call out to my Savior, for only He can rescue

NEEDING GOD

My God, my all-knowing God
    I really need to hear from You
There's something going on
    And I don't know what to do
It feels so very ugly
    And I really can't explain
I do know that I am suffering
    For I feel tremendous pain

I need a word from You, Father
    Please tell me what I'm going through
I thought I was doing the right thing
    The way I praised and worshipped You
Something still is so very wrong, Lord
    Which one of these was my bad choice?
Did I listen to the longings of my flesh
    And refused to hearken to Your Voice

Help me to correct my vision
    I know there's something I need to see
Like giving my battles all to Jesus
    Then watching every enemy flee
Show me how to renounce all fear and stress
    That has caused my loneliness
Please embrace my heart, dear God
    As I move towards healing, from brokenness

Let Your Spirit empty me completely
    So only with Jesus I will sup
Take my spirit and my soul
    So Your anointing can fill me up
I want to be like Your sheep that know Your voice
    So I'll hear You when You talk
Create a path of life for me
    So with You, I'll only walk

PRAY

When a friend is hurting deep inside
And comforting words are hard to say
The only thing to be done for them
Is find a quiet place to pray

As a young child becomes very ill
Or a senior is facing his last day
Encouraging hope and strength will come
When only for them we stop and pray

Lost inside ourselves, feeling empty
Searching desperately to find our way
We go to a place that's familiar to us
Our secret closet where we pray

Most of our weeping is only at night
Tossing and turning where we lay
Inner storms are constantly rising
We only find peace by kneeling to pray

As the hour of our Lord drew nigh
For on earth He could no longer stay
He poured His heart out to God above
When He went to Gethsemane to pray

So often, circumstances will come our way
But our spirits can be lifted everyday
Knowing we gave everything to God
Because we set aside the time to pray

REDEDICATION

You know, he walked away from Jesus one day
Just decided he wanted to do things his way
Basically, he thought the world would be the same
Until Satan arrived with a brand new game
You see, he started out by taking him on a ride
First stops were rebellion, lust and pride
Then he dropped by depression, envy and strife
Satan was deceiving him and running his life

He got in big trouble, it looked pretty bad
Then Satan claimed him with all the tricks he had
The situation became serious, he was paying a cost
He was too bound to see that Satan had become his boss
There was a turn of events, that happened so quick
His life was slipping away, he became very, very sick
He needed some attention; someone to be around
He kept a search ongoing, nobody could be found

Things were really bad, his body was so weak
While drowning in despair, he heard his conscience speak
"You were doing fine, until that day you left"
"You pushed away your help, trying to do it all yourself"
He realized he was dying, there was nothing he could do
No doctors or no medicine could every pull him through
As he saw the life he lived, passing through his head
He said the "Sinner's Prayer" on his dying bed

Jesus came back to him, for He was never really gone
He most graciously forgave him, for all he had done wrong
He felt a warm sensation, his pains he didn't feel
You see, Jesus had never left his heart, the Holy Spirit is our seal
If you feel your life is empty, there's something missing there
Start reading the Word of God and say a "child-like" prayer
Don't let the enemy tell you; you've waited far too late
As long as you are living, you can still rededicate

SOUL SURRENDER

Let's take a spiritual dive
      Spiraling way down deep within
To a place we seldom tarry
      Exactly where all life begins
To the spot where storms arise
      Needing nurturing and care
Is it a lonely place? I think not
      For the Holy Spirit is dwelling there
There's a stillness there, but listen
      For the Spirit will be your Guide
Close your eyes and merely meditate
      Feel all the movement that's inside
Allow the Spirit to draw you closer
      So to you, your Father will come near
Trust the guidance that is given
      For doubting will only cause you to fear
There's nothing for you to say
      For human words are unspeakable
Because here the Spirit makes intercession
      You're at the core of your own soul
Quietly and slowly you feel the conviction
      Then comes your strangling soulful cry
For the need of your Savior's help
      To cleanse you, lest you die
A spiritual awakening is upon you
      Soul and spirit have now conferred
Being submerged in living water
      Finally, your will you have surrendered

STEPPING ASIDE

When you know you're in the right and the other person's wrong
As you explain to them your point, it seems impossible to get along
Rather than lose you self-control, you take no stand and swallow pride
By letting them have their say,
      By just merely stepping aside

You've been unjustly accused, knowing the situation isn't fair
No one will hear you out, because they really don't even care
It's a devastating blow, for on you someone has truly lied
Can you give this over the Jesus?
      Say no more, just step aside

To some you may appear weak; you'll hear a lot of voices mumble
But in the sight of God, He sees that your heart is meek and humble
You won't have to bear this cross alone, you'll have Jesus at your side
The situation will be resolved,
      Because you chose to step aside

Life will produce many trials, filled with unexpected pain
By using ungodly tactics, there'll be nothing for you to gain
You must learn from your humble Master, letting go of things you've tried
Knowing that He will produce the victory
      You can courageously step aside

THAT DAY

I remember the day
        When all the attacks began
The day I lost my focus
        On God's eternal plan
His words, His grace, His love
        All the promises that I knew
Gone because of my choices
        To do what I wanted to do

I remember days of sorrow
        Because peace could not be found
Sin had become my ruling master
        I felt to far gone to turn around
Couldn't understand why I constantly cried
        For they were not the tears of joy
The constant anger, pain and rage
        All a part of the enemy's ploy

I remember the day that I hit bottom
        It was a long and torturous drop
It was the furthest I could go
        For the world to me had stopped
Desperately my mine began to search
        For the things I knew were good
The answers slowly began to come
        All of a sudden I understood
I remember I said a prayer
        Asking God to please help me
I prayed for complete deliverance
        From this clutching enemy
I realized that God truly loved me
        Because of His unselfish, incredible Gift
His begotten Son, the resurrected One
        He made my spirit lift

I remember the day
        When all reality came back to me
The day that Jesus broke the shackles
        The day my soul was finally free
I'll always remember that day
        Because He removed the pain and strife
The thing that I will remember the most
        It was the day that Jesus saved my life

THE BATTLE

Frustrations, depression, bad memories of all kinds
There's something tormenting me, deep inside of my mind
It's a war that is raging and raging so fast
It is difficult to determine the present from the past
It's an invisible enemy, his spirits attack
It gets harder and harder for me to fight back
His arrows are poison, his lies seem so real
He's trying to destroy my mind and my will
I need some protection, I need it right now
I've got to call on Jesus, He'll help me somehow
He'll send the Holy Spirit to fight the battle for me
He'll reveal His great truths to insure victory
Many battles will be waged, many wars will be fought
Many lessons to be learned, but my mind will be taught
That the fight in my head for me is a test
To destroy the enemy's yoke and bring out my best

THE JOURNEY

I am at a particular place
    It has surroundings that I don't know
I'm not suppose to be here
    There's a reason that I must go
I seek my freedom from the enemy
    So many things here just aren't right
There's a movement in my spirit
    Telling my soul to take its flight
Which direction shall I go?
    Will someone for me lead the way?
Something dreadful is really scaring me
    Telling my soul that I should stay
What lies ahead for me is uncertain
    Staying is a chance I can't afford
I'm leaving, not looking back
    For I'm going towards the Lord
I have finally broken free
    Now there's a sea that I must cross
As I cross over, I'll say goodbye
    To the world that had me lost
I am standing now bewildered
    At a place apart from everything

I find peace because God is with me
    And to Him I give thanks and sing
As I continue on this journey
    There are no thoughts of what I need
I'll trust and depend on Jehovah
    For as He promised, He clothes and feeds
In traveling, now I press forward
    Experiencing uncertainty at every turn
I have faith in God to guide me
    For there are lessons here I must learn
My spirit being so elated
    The sensation awesome, and wonderful

Up ahead is what God has promised me
    A life rewarding and beautiful
I've become a part of His family
    Never, ever again will I be alone
This was a long and tedious journey
    But God has finally brought me home

THE VOICE

Have you every listened to the Voice within?
    Saying, "Talk to me, talk to me" over and over again
Have you ever wanted to cry and utter words that you couldn't say?
    And the Voice within said, "Go ahead, I'll listen anyway"
You take a deep breath, dry your eyes and confess
    You start crying again, there's so much on your chest
The Voice tells you, "Cry, cry, cry until you're through"
    "Because when you're done crying, I'm going to forgive you"
But then the Voice says, "Have you told Me everything
    Or is there some things you want to keep?"
The Voice says, "I want it all"
    Once again you start to weep
One more try, you give Him the rest
    The good, the bad, the worst and even your best
Surrendering everything, all of you
    The Voice says, "It's okay, I gave Myself too"
Now that you've given Him all that's within
    The Voice kindly says, "I'm your newfound Friend"
To keep this friendship, you wonder, "What must I do?"
    The Voice plainly says, "Love everyone as I have loved you.
Now that you've learned to recognize His Voice
    It's time for a decision, you must make your choice
Should you chose to follow Him, you'll have a guarantee
    Life after death, with Him throughout all eternity

WHERE ARE YOU?

As I was looking out my window
I just began to stare
Asking a very serious question
God, are You really out there?
If You're out there God
I've got something to say
I guess what I am really doing
I'm really trying to pray
I can't see or touch You, God
And that's really hard for me
But I want this thing called faith
That salvation that is free
I want my spirit unleashed
So in my heart I will believe
Plus I need Your gift of grace
That You say all can receive
I meet people who love Jesus
They all seem to really care
The look that's on their faces say
You really are out there
They have a radiant glow
And have very strongly said
Any faith that has no works
Will be most surely dead

They speak of how Jesus died
A death for them and for me
They say His real purpose for coming
Was to set the captives free
They say my coming to You
Must be built on love and trust
Most importantly they said
Reading Your Word is a must
I think it's time for me, God
To take a very good look
At all the things that are written
In Your most precious Holy Book
I've heard I'll get connected
To the true and only Vine
My spirit will be quickened
My past left far behind
I'm feeling confident God
That all this is for real
There's a very profound meaning
To everything I feel
It's the reality of belonging
To Someone I know who cares
Within the deepest part of my heart God
I know You really are there

REMEMBRANCE

REMEMBRANCE

Webster's Dictionary says that **"remembrance"** is the state of bearing in mind. The ability to remember. An act of recalling to mind. A memory of a person, thing or event.

How often have we had memories that encouraged us to keep going? Think about it – there have been individuals; i.e., pastors, speakers, singers, etc. who lifted our spirits to the point that we wanted to draw closer and closer to God. Over the years, we remember individuals who walked by faith, proclaiming victory and had the surety of Jesus Christ in their lives. Individuals whose lives were sometimes tainted with various trials and tribulations and their faith never wavered.

The patriarchs, disciples, apostles, prophets and saints of old exclusively lived their lives expressing their love, trust, and faith in the will of God. Many other individuals throughout history have showed their remarkable unrelenting trust in God. This final section highlights several individuals who through their unswerving faith in an incomprehensible God, overcame all obstacles, to fulfill all of His purposes, by His incalculable power and grace.

Grace be to you from God the Father through Jesus Christ.

A LEADER FOR GOD

There was a decree to kill every male Israelite child
    He was laid in a basket and placed in the Nile
No one ever knew that he was in the water
    He was found by a princess; she was Pharaoh's daughter
She drew him out as if a prized had been won
    To the Egyptian palace he went, raised as her son
His acts and his deeds, he thought was the plan
    Until that dreadful day came when he killed a man
He fled that great land, he left in a hurry
    Never wanting to return, but that's only part of the story
In the wilderness he stayed, a number of years
    A shepherd he became, forgetting his fears
The Spirit gently stirred him to find his lost lamb
    In the wilderness, he searched with his staff in his hand
Looking around, something caused him to stop
    He thought, "Looks like something's burning there on the mountain top"
The desire to know within him did push
    When he arrived at the top, all he saw was a bush
He became filled with awe, as he looked all around
    The fiery bush said, "You're on holy ground"
"You're going back to Egypt, you're going for Me"
    "My people are held captive and I want them free.
You can never tell which person God will chose
    If you walk in obedience, you'll never lose
To God this man became one of the best
    Being redeemed though a murderer, his name was Moses

Scripture Reading: Exodus 2 to Deuteronomy 34

DISCIPLESHIP

We sometimes find people who think only of themselves
But the disciples of Jesus were a remarkable twelve
With Jesus, they often walked and talked wherever they went
They learned the true reason for which He was sent
There was James and Andrew, who were fisher of men to be
They quickly dropped their nets when they heard, "Follow Me"
Although Peter denied Him before three cries of the cock
He proved to be strong as his name, Cephas, the "Rock"
John, who has a heart as beautiful as a dove
Became known as the disciple that Jesus did love
Judas Iscariot was different than the rest of them
He had the wrong spirit and would soon betray Him
He spoke to the remaining as He arose up to God
Giving them instructions to preach the Gospel abroad
A disciple is someone we all should become
To proclaim the Good News of God's only Son
It's a job that is not so easily done
But the rewards are so great, they compare to none
You'll speak of a Savior, who will dwell in your heart
Explain that He's someone you can't live apart
You'll show to them His words that ring so true
And by His grace they will see He lives inside you

Scripture Reading: The New Testament Gospels of the Holy Bible

HE HEALS

Emotional scars
    Pains so deep, they're unreal
Mind and body so crushed
    They need to be healed
There's great desire to stop
    All the hurt and the tears
Cause you feel trapped like the woman
    Who had the issue for years
Being an outcast and with no help
    She knew she would die
Then she heard of a Healer
    Said she's give Him a try
If she could just get to Him
    Her faith said it wouldn't take much
And if she got close enough
    Maybe just one touch
She was ashamed, but determined
    But she didn't cry out at all
Her spirit told her to go
    Even if it meant she must crawl

She pushed herself forward
    Hiding her face as she went
Pressing forward, she saw Him
    Touched the end of His garment
He felt what she did
    Wanted to know who it was
She came trembling before Him
    And pleaded her cause
He had the look of compassion
    And to her He did tell
"Be of good cheer
    Your faith made you well"
As you are dealing with issues
    And there seems to be no relief

When you must go to the Healer
    You must go in belief
Believe that His work is guaranteed
    For He has nothing to sell
It is only by your faith
    That He will make you well

Scripture Reading: Matthew 9:20-23; Mark 5:25-34; Luke 8:43-48

HER DESTINY

They were of no blood relation
Ruth was only a dedicated wife
She was a Gentile, not a Hebrew
For she was born a Moabite
She was married to Naomi's son
Now a part of the family's clan
Naomi was living in Ruth's country
Because of the famine in her land
Naomi lost her husband
Her sons died shortly after
Left with only her daughter-in-laws
She felt robbed of joy and laughter
Faced with loneliness and pain
She told the young women each goodbye
But Ruth clung close to Naomi's side
Said , "Where thou diest, will I die"
Ruth returned to Naomi's country
The famine had ended in the land
There was uncertainty set before them
But God had a purpose and a plan
The Lord knew what Ruth must go through
So she received the protection of His shield

Ruth began working around Naomi's relative
    For she was gleaning in his field
God began to move in Naomi's spirit
    She spoke words to Ruth that were very wise
Ruth obeyed all that Naomi said
    And she found favor in Boaz's eyes
Because of her trust and dedication
    The love for Naomi that she carried
Boaz began to love Ruth deeply
    Until united as one, they were married
As you read through the Holy Scriptures
    And check the lineage through and through

There was a child born whose name was Jesse
    To the family of Boaz and of Ruth
Then Jesse begat King David
    From this lineage as we read
Of which came the only Begotten One
    Our Savior Jesus, the Promised Seed

Scripture Reading: The book of Ruth; Matthew 1:5-6

KING DAVID

He was the smallest of all of Jesse's sons
David was merely a shepherd boy
But He possessed a very special gift
For it was in God he found his joy
He learned to trust God in all things
A reverence he had from the very start
As the anointing was placed upon his life
He became a man after God's own heart

As this calling was set before him
David knew that his God would lead
He held on to all of the promises
And the prophecy of the future Seed
He fought so very bravely
Knowing that his God was always around
Defeating armies and capturing cities
He even brought a giant to the ground

There was something that David wanted
Was it a part of God's eternal plan?
For David's flesh took complete control of him
Yielding to the lust that's within man
David committed very sinful acts
Thought he'd get away oh so free
But God saw all that David did
He could never let this thing just be
God sent a messenger to David
The words were so very strong
Exposing all the terrible things
That David had done wrong
Out of the darkness, his sins lit up
The exposure right before his eyes
He had to turn and stand before God
David knew there'd be no more lies
Knowing his was before the Master
He cried out in true repentance
As God so lovingly forgave him
There still came the consequence

There were a lot of dear things lost
A devastating price that David paid
But all the promises were fulfilled
Regarding the covenant that God had made
David was called, anointed and blessed
Right from the very start
God stayed with him through thick and thin
A man truly after God's own heart

Scripture Reading: 2nd Samuel 11-12:1-25; Psalm 51

THE APOSTLE

He sought out to persecute every Christian Jew
    In his mind he thought it was the right thing to do
He led his attacks on every Christian there was
    Thinking that his fight was for a just cause
The City of Damascus was where he was going
    Something changed on the road
A bright light was showing
    The light was so bright
Not a person could see
    The Voice said, "Saul, Saul, why persecutest thou Me"
After talking with Jesus, through the brightest of light
    He sent him on his journey; though his eyes had no sight
With the Spirit upon him,
    His old job was through
Being led by his Master, he knew what to do

He now preached the Gospel, the Gospel of Christ
    It didn't matter to him, whatever the price
He faced persecution, he never sought fame
    He worked only for God, in Jesus' name
He traveled abroad preaching the Word

    The truth of our Lord had to be heard
To Philippi, Galatia and Corinth he went
    It was only by the Spirit that he was sent
In prison he spent the last of his days
    He still preached the Word so that souls could be saved
He never looked backed from that Damascus Road call
    He served God til his death,. The Apostle was Paul

Scripture Reading: Acts 7:54-8:3; Acts 9:1-31;13:1-28:31; Romans and The Epistles

THE DREAMER

Being truly loved by his father
He received a coat of many colors
This caused sever jealously
Among some of his brothers
He was ridiculed for his dreams
Never having the upper hand
But God was always with him
He had a purpose and a plan

He did his brothers no wrong
But they treated him terribly
They took away his coat
And sold him into slavery
Although rejected and alone
Things appeared to be very dim
He still worshipped the Lord
As always, God was with him

In Egypt, at Potiphar's house he now lived
Becoming the second person in command
In all that he did, he prospered
He became known in the land
His master's wife lusted for him
But from her he did run
She told a vicious lie to her husband
Who placed him in prison
Being alone once again
He became friends with the jailer
Still holding on to his dreams

In the Lord's eyes he found favor
Blessed with a gift to interpret
Any dream, whether good or bad
Knowing that God was the revealer
He interpreted those the king had

Taken from prison by the king
Again, placed second in command
Working diligently to save a country
From the famine in the land
His family began to need food
For without it they would die
It was to Egypt they must go
To see what they could buy

They made two journeys for the goods
Each time pleading their cause
It was the second time that they came
He revealed who he was
As they embraced one another
It was only love that he could give
Told them all to come back to Egypt
It was there they would live
This was Joseph, the loving son of Israel
Who dreamed of fortune and fame
But the plan for his life
Involved humility and shame
We must learn as Joseph did
For he finally understood
That what others may mean for bad
The Almighty God will mean for good

Scripture Reading: Genesis 37-50

THREE DETERMINED MEN

They were employed by the king
        Handling the affairs of the land
Living a life in captivity
        Doing the best that they can
They feared and loved God
        Faithfully worshipped Him each day
The only time they knelt
        Was when they bowed to God to pray

In Babylon, a city of idolatry
        Sin was practiced all around
The king built an image of gold
        For everyone to bow down
The young men didn't give any thought
        To all the things that they saw
Because they knew their God of Israel
        And from His strength they would draw

The king gave them an ultimatum
        Something for each of them to try
Bow down and worship the image
        Or by the furnace they would die
They refused to drop to their knees
        And the order to burn them was sent
The fire was made extremely hot
        Into the furnace, the three of them went

While the fire was ablaze
    The king peered through the door
He was looking for the burning three
    But to His surprise, he saw four
Upon removal they were unharmed
    But out of the furnace only came three
Astonished, the king wondered
    How could this possibly be?

The king then realized
    That the young men were not alone
Their God had sent an angel
    For the protection of His own
They were immediately released
    They're lives no longer at any risk
The king spoke sincerely, that
    No other God can deliver like this

Life really tries to turn us
    In many, many different ways
But regardless to what may happen
    We must still give God our praise
These three young men didn't waver
    Refusing to go with the world's flow
We'll always know them as,
    Shadrach, Meshach and Abednego

Scripture Reading: Daniel 3

WHAT ADAM HAD

There's a longing deep within,
    A yearning that makes you sad
It's to be so close to God,
    To be able to feel what Adam had
Things were in perfect order,
    There was nothing but beauty to behold
Life held nothing but splendor,
    Never emptiness of soul
How could something so perfect,
    Change in one sinful day
Perfect order was interrupted,
    In such a deceitful way
Satan initiated the drama;
    Directed the entire scene
His rebellion was really towards God,
    Pride had made him just that mean
It caused man and woman to hide,
    Afraid to face their own Creator
Knowledge of fear set upon them,
    They knew they see Him sooner of later
As they tried to cover up,
    Completely naked and feeling bad

Life had taken a drastic turn,
>	It was not longer what they had
Just imagine how it must have felt,
>	For God to walk the earth with man
To think that it was all predestined,
>	For His will, His purpose, His plan
The sin committed in the garden,
>	Brought separation to us all
It took Jesus to come from heaven,
>	To save us from Adam's fall
As the end of this age will come,
>	And Satan will be brought to his final end

Sweet victory with triumph over evil,
>	Because righteousness will win
Our Savior will come to meet us,
>	Our souls will be joyful and glad
Once again there will be harmony,
>	And we'll have what Adam had

Genesis 1:26 – 3:24

CPSIA information can be obtained
at www.ICGtesting.com
Printed in the USA
FFHW010759030719
53380496-59066FF